The Magic of
Sleep

Written and illustrated by
Vicky Woodgate

Author and Illustrator Vicky Woodgate
Concept and Design Vicky Woodgate

Editor Fay Evans
Consultant Vicki Dawson
US Editor Megan Douglass
Jacket Designer Sonny Flynn
Managing Art Editor Diane Peyton Jones
Senior Production Editor Rob Dunn
Production Controller Francesca Sturiale
Jacket Coordinator Issy Walsh
Creative Director Helen Senior
Publishing Director Sarah Larter

First American Edition, 2021
Published in the United States by DK Publishing
1450 Broadway, Suite 801, New York, NY 10018

A catalog record for this book
is available from the Library of Congress.
ISBN: 978-0-7440-2654-2

Printed and bound in China

For the curious
www.dk.com

MIX
Paper from
responsible sources
FSC™ C018179

The BIGGEST ever pajama party in the world had 2,000 guests!

CONTENTS

4-5
What is sleep?

6-7
Sleeping positions

8-9
Larks and owls

10-11
The body

12-13
Stages of sleep

14-15
Dreams

16-17
Nightmares

18-19
History, myths, and legends

20-21
Sleep through history

22-23
Beds through time

24-27
Myths and legends

28-29
The night sky

30-31
Humans and sleep

32-33
Night work

34-35
How and where

36-37
How much sleep?

38-39
The map of sleep

40-41
Sleep in nature

42-43
Sky

44-45
Land

46-47
Underground

48-49
Underwater

50-51
Who's awake?

52-53
Sleep in numbers

54-55
Plants

56-57
Tips for better sleep

58-59
True or false

60-61
Mindfulness

62-63
Dream journal

64-67
Practical tips

68-69
Glossary

70-71
Index

72
Acknowledgments

WHAT IS SLEEP?

Meet our sleep guide

Cats LOVE to snooze, so who better to guide you through the magical and mysterious world of sleep than your very own sleep expert, Mimi Cat.

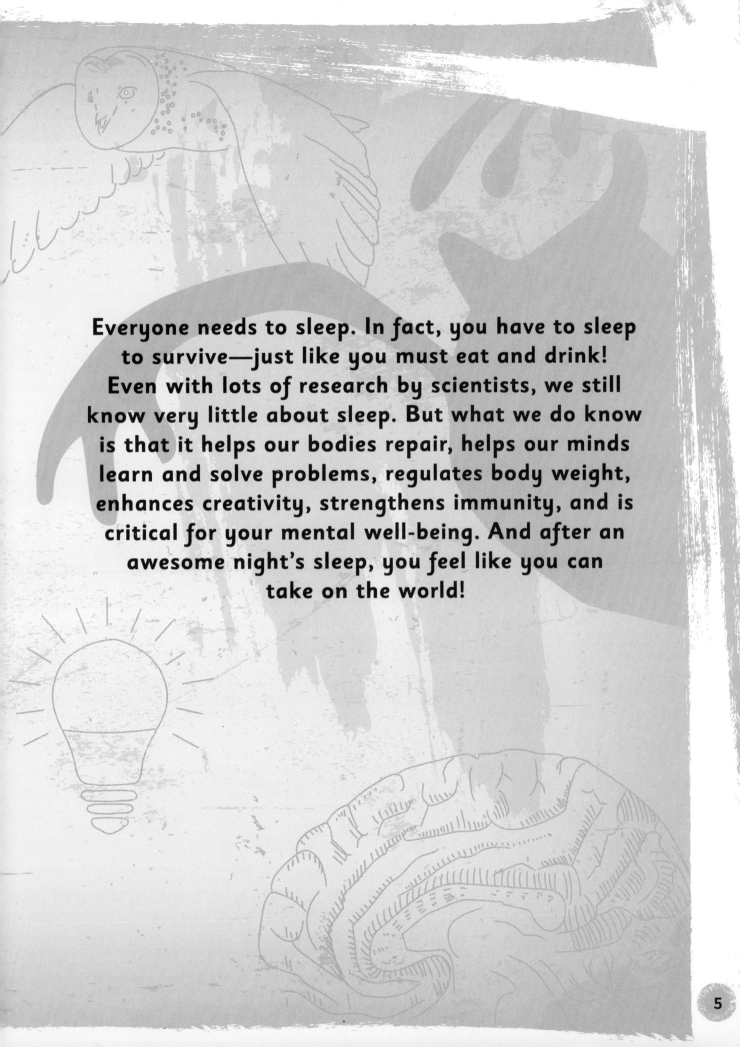

Everyone needs to sleep. In fact, you have to sleep to survive—just like you must eat and drink! Even with lots of research by scientists, we still know very little about sleep. But what we do know is that it helps our bodies repair, helps our minds learn and solve problems, regulates body weight, enhances creativity, strengthens immunity, and is critical for your mental well-being. And after an awesome night's sleep, you feel like you can take on the world!

SLEEPING POSITIONS

How do you sleep? Curled up in a ball or sprawled all over the bed? Most of us sleep in one of the common positions below (though you might change positions many times throughout the night!). Which one matches you best?

Soldier

On your back with arms by your sides, this position helps stop face lines but can make you snore!

Starfish

What a bed hog! This is a good position for your back but can also make you snore.

Log

Sleep like a log and enjoy a peaceful night sleeping on your side.

Discover how many people share your sleeping position*...

 8%

5%

 14%

6

*Of 1,000 people polled.

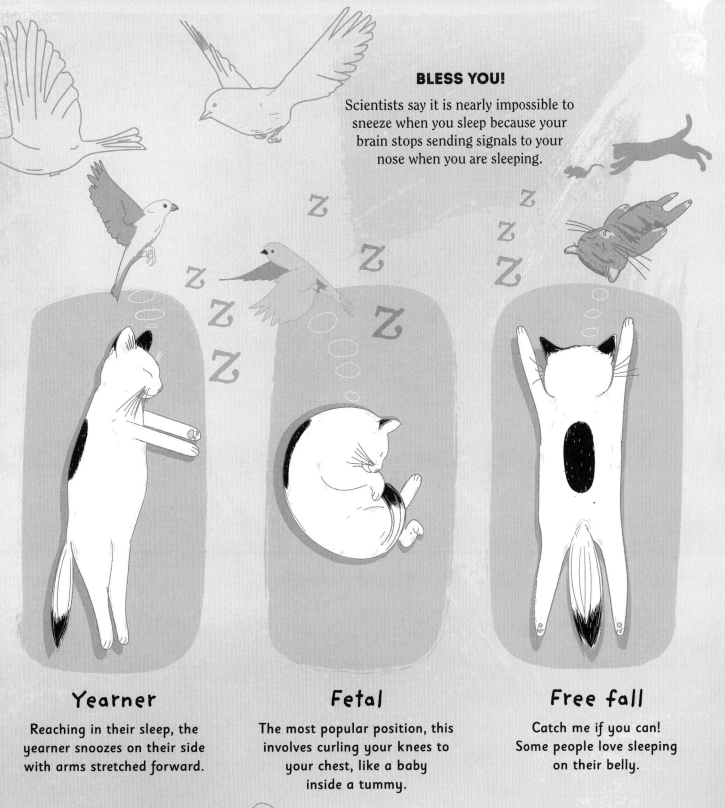

BLESS YOU!

Scientists say it is nearly impossible to sneeze when you sleep because your brain stops sending signals to your nose when you are sleeping.

Yearner

Reaching in their sleep, the yearner snoozes on their side with arms stretched forward.

Fetal

The most popular position, this involves curling your knees to your chest, like a baby inside a tummy.

Free fall

Catch me if you can! Some people love sleeping on their belly.

13%

41%

7%

LARKS AND OWLS

Do you spring out of bed first thing in the morning? Bright-eyed and bushy-tailed, ready for the day? Or do you pull the covers over your head looking for more snooze time? Most of us fall into specific sleep pattern groups and our genetics play a role in which group we belong to.

"I love getting up early!"

Circadian rhythm

A 24-hour internal clock running in the background of our brains! Responding to light and dark, it tells us when we should go to sleep and when to wake up.

The body clock

20%
Lark

Lark types are more alert and work harder in the mornings, but get tired earlier in the evening.

"I like getting up late and love going to bed early!"

60%
Hummingbird

Hummingbirds are a mixture of both lark and owl types and can switch between the two patterns. Current research suggests there may even be subgroups within this chronotype!

Percentages are a rough estimate based on a range of studies.

SWIFTS AND WOODCOCKS!

A chronotype defines your sleep pattern! We know of three, but more research is being uncovered and there are suggestions there may be more, called swifts and woodcocks!

"I like staying up late."

No Change

Studies suggest that if you were born a lark or an owl, it is almost impossible to change from one to another.

20%
Owl

Owl types struggle to wake up in the morning and tend to function much better later in the day.

QUIZ
What are you?

1. When it's time to wake up do you ...

a. Spring out of bed—no alarm needed!
b. Press the snooze button, just a couple more minutes ...
c. Pull the covers over your head and ignore the alarm.

2. Your typical bedtime ...

a. PJs are on, bedtime book read, and ready for lights off.
b. Finish homework, dinner, watch TV—oops, time for bed already!
c. Still awake after lights out; there is SO much to think about!

3. Do you feel sleepy in the daytime?

a. No.
b. Sometimes.
c. Yes, especially in the morning.

4. What is your favorite time to eat?

a. Breakfast—you are starving!
b. Midmorning snack!
c. Late night munch!

5. It's the weekend; when do you wake up?

a. Nice and early, ready for the day.
b. A little extra snooze, it IS the weekend after all!
c. Don't wake me before lunch.

Answer:
Mostly As   Lark
Mostly Bs   Hummingbird
Mostly Cs   Owl

THE BODY

What happens to our bodies when we sleep? Do we just turn ourselves off? The body can become quite busy while we are peacefully snoozing. It moves into maintenance mode, recovering from damage and protecting itself against future illness and injury.

Eyes

Have you ever seen someone's eyes dart back and forth under their lids when they sleep? This is called REM—Rapid Eye Movement—which happens when we dream.

Brain

Your brain stays active when you drift off, entering four different stages, each lasting roughly 90 minutes.

"I ALWAYS get my beauty sleep."

Stomach

Your digestive system slows down at night. Not getting enough sleep can affect our hormones, making us feel hungry.

Kidney

The kidneys filter toxins from your blood and make urine. When you sleep, the kidneys slow down but continue to filter potentially harmful substances to keep you healthy.

Skin

Growth hormones are released while you sleep, helping your body grow and repair itself. Cool fact alert: this is where the term "get your beauty sleep" comes from!

TEMPERATURE

Why do we love to snuggle under the covers? It's because our body temperature drops when we snooze.

Lymph nodes

If you don't get enough sleep, your body produces fewer proteins which signal your immune system to respond to problems in the body. This may cause you to be more likely to catch colds, coughs, and viruses!

Bones

Studies have shown that bones actually grow when you sleep, so if you want strong, healthy bones, get those Zzzs in!

You break wind when you sleep!

Muscles

During REM sleep, your eyes move rapidly but your muscles become paralyzed. This is nature's way of keeping us from acting out our dreams and hurting ourselves!

CATCH ME IF YOU CAN

Have you ever felt like you are falling only to suddenly jolt awake? This is called a hypnic jerk, but don't worry—it's nothing more than an involuntary twitch.

Stage one

In the first stage of sleep, our brainwaves slow down. Our heartbeat also slows, and our muscles start to relax as we slowly drift off.

At this stage it is very easy to be woken up.

It is a short phase lasting up to 10 minutes.

HORMONES

The hormone melatonin guides our body clock—we produce more when it gets dark. Melatonin not only helps us sleep, it protects our body cells from molecules that can damage us. These are called free radicals.

Stage two

As we enter stage two, our heartbeat continues to slow, as does our breathing, and our muscles become even more relaxed. Our body temperature drops and our brains produce sleep spindles—rapid rhythmic brain waves that occur every minute or so.

It is still fairly easy to wake up at this point.

BRAIN

Rapid bursts of electrical activity are crucial for your brain to transfer short-term memories to long-term ones.

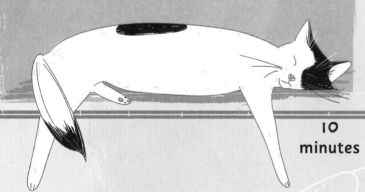

10 minutes

First sleep cycle timeline

30 minutes

STAGES OF SLEEP

Once we fall asleep, it takes an average 90 minutes to go through all the stages. An ideal night consists of about five to six cycles (depending on age and individual). As the clock ticks, the amount of time we spend in each stage shifts. Our deep sleep becomes less and the REM sleep where we dream lasts longer.

Stage three

We have now entered a deep sleep and it is difficult to wake up at this point. Our body has moved to the repair stage. There is increased blood flow to the muscles, tissue can grow and repair, bones grow and mend, and our immunity is boosted.

SNOOZE TIME

A child will spend an average 40% of their childhood asleep!

You are more likely to sleepwalk at this stage.

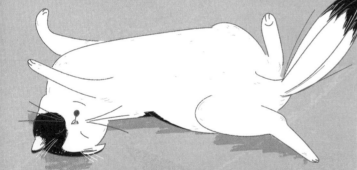

REM Sleep

After about 60-70 minutes, we move into the next stage, known as REM sleep—Rapid Eye Movement. Our brain activity increases, breathing becomes faster, the heart rate raises, and our leg and arm muscles become paralyzed.

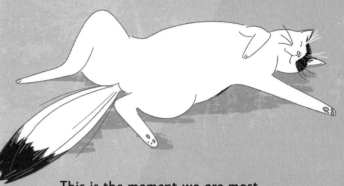

This is the moment we are most likely to dream, processing thoughts, emotions, and experiences.

REM

REM sleep encourages the brain to develop long-term memory, learning, and imagination. Babies spend more time in REM sleep than any other age group—smart tots!

Sleep Cycles

After moving through our first cycle and completing REM stage, we move back into stages one and two and start the process all over again. With longer REM sleep stages as the cycles progress we dream longer.

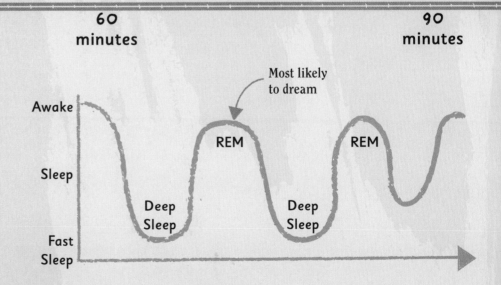

60 minutes

90 minutes

Most likely to dream

Awake

REM

REM

Sleep

Deep Sleep

Deep Sleep

Fast Sleep

12% of us dream in black and white! When we do dream in color it tends to be in soft pastel colors.

Left-handed

If you are left-handed you are likely to have more fantastical and lucid dreams than right-handed people.

What we see

Dreams are influenced by our own experiences, however some dream themes are common with many, including being chased, falling, feeling frozen on the spot, and flying.

How often

We dream about 3 to 6 times a night, ranging from 5 to 20 minutes for each dream. That means we could dream an average of 6 years in a lifetime.

?

95% of our dreams are forgotten by the time we get out of bed.

Animals

Animals dream, too! Studies have shown they also go through stages of sleep including REM sleep, the stage when we are most likely to dream.

Memories

Dreaming can help you learn and develop long-term memories.

DREAMS

Everybody dreams. They can be funny, sad, or just plain weird! We don't really know all the reasons we dream, but it could be a way for all the information we gather in our brains to be deciphered and processed.

INVENTIONS

Some of the best ideas have come from dreams. Larry Page came up with the idea for Google while dreaming!

Triggers

Nightmares can be triggered by anything—something you have seen or experienced, a scary TV show, a horror story, computer game, or even just a shadow on the wall!

Emotions

What we think about before we go to sleep can affect our dreams, too. The upside to having a nightmare is that you normally feel much better after! This is because your brain has processed the worrying emotion that triggered the bad dream.

Nightmare vs night terror

Night terrors are a bit different from nightmares. These experiences are normally found in stage 2-3 of sleep—the NREM (non-rapid eye movement) stage—and can include physical actions like shouting, moving, and jumping out of bed! We are still fast asleep in these episodes.

Fears and worries

If you keep having nightmares, see if you can speak to someone you trust. They may be able to help you discover what might be worrying you.

NIGHTMARES

Stress, fear, anxiety, and sadness—all these feelings can fuel disturbing dreams. Having a bad dream can wake you up and make you feel scared. It is ok to feel frightened! Dreams can feel very authentic, but they are not real, it is just our amazing brains and imagination working through our emotions and experiences.

HISTORY, MYTHS, AND LEGENDS

Adored

Ancient Egyptians worshipped cats (of course). Bastet, the goddess of cats, was thought to be the soul of Isis, the goddess of the moon.

It's fascinating what different cultures and faiths through the ages thought about sleep. Many civilizations believed their gods communicated with them in their slumber. Countless people believed that dreams could predict the future! Mythical and magical legends surrounding sleep were passed down through the generations.

What we actually slept on and where we slept also changed. It was common for groups of people to sleep together, though that changed to more solitary sleep over the years. Even our sleep patterns shifted through time ...

The Mesopotamians

7,000 years ago, Mesopotamians believed that dreams could predict the future. They would record them on clay tablets, creating the first dream diaries.

Dream tablet

Alcmaeon of Croton

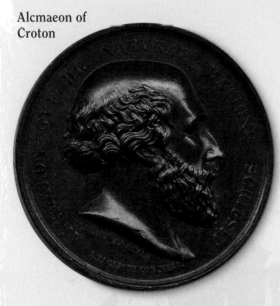

The Ancient Greeks

In 450 BCE, the Greek medical theorist Alcmaeon of Croton was convinced that sleep was a spell of unconsciousness bought on by blood withdrawing from the surface of the body. Yet by the 19th century, medical doctors speculated sleep was the result of too much blood in the brain!

Bastet

The Egyptians

In 800 BCE, the ancient Egyptians constructed huge temples to worship the goddess Isis, the goddess of the moon. Many would gather together to decipher their dreams, believing they were messages from the gods.

SLEEP THROUGH HISTORY

Many cultures through time had very different ideas about sleep. Ancient Egyptians cherished and embraced it. Medieval Christians were fearful, believing themselves to be in mortal peril as they slumbered. Even what time we slept adapted over the years, moving from two periods of sleep to the now more common single continuous snooze ...

Biphasic sleep

Before the invention of electricity, many people followed a two-part sleeping pattern as they would run out of daylight! They would go to bed at dusk, waking in the middle of the night to eat, read, do chores and even visit friends, then resuming their sleep for a few hours before day break.

Monophasic sleep

With the invention of artificial light and more controlled work patterns after the industrial revolution, more people adopted a single sleep phase of eight hours. This continues today in most countries around the world.

Rich vs poor

People from richer backgrounds were able to stay up later as they could afford more candles!

Let there be light

The dark could be a dangerous place in the past, and when artificial light was introduced, it changed the world. From gas lighting the streets in the 1790s to the invention of the light bulb 100 years later, it opened up the night. Despite this, there are about a billion people today that still do not have electric light at home.

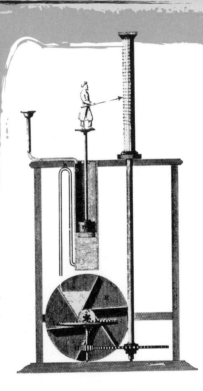

Devilish thoughts

Medieval Christians thought that they were vulnerable to the devil while asleep and that he could invade their dreams.

A wake up device was invented in 1882 which involved dropping heavy objects on your head to wake you up—OUCH!

(Luckily it didn't catch on!)

BONG!

In 250 BCE Ctesibius the Ancient Greek engineer invented the first alarm clock—using a pointer device on a water clock to drop pebbles on a gong.

BEDS THROUGH TIME

For thousands of years, people slept on piles of dead plants and animal furs. Gradually, bed frames and mattresses became more widely used and the beds themselves more comfortable, eventually becoming the cozy bed you'll sleep in tonight!

Feathers have been used for hundreds of years to stuff bedding.

10,000 BCE
At this time, people slept together on giant beds made of layers of leaves, including ferns.

Roman day bed

1000 BCE
Persians used goat skins filled with water to sleep on—the first ever water beds!

3200 BCE
Ancient Northern European tribes slept on beds made of raised blocks of stone. Ouch!

700 BCE– 450 CE
Wealthy Romans loved beds and had one for every occasion—for eating, sleeping, and entertaining!

2000 BCE
Rich Egyptians slept on wooden bed frames covered in gold with carved animal feet. The head rests, however, were REALLY hard!

STRAW MATTRESS
During the Middle Ages, many slept on straw stuffed sacking. This is where the popular saying "hit the hay" came from.

The world's oldest mattress was discovered in the Sibudu Cave in South Africa. It is thought to be over 77,000 years old!

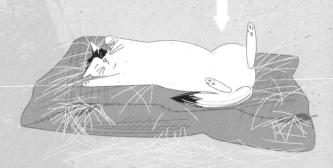

Animal feet

Wooden Egyptian head rest

THE KING OF BEDS

Louis XIV of France LOVED beds so much that he owned 413! Many were decorated with gold, silver, and pearls.

Bedsprings

Victorian bed

BUNK BEDS

Originally popular with the military, they became popular in modern homes partially because of how fun they were to sleep on!

1400

In Europe simple wooden bed frames became more common. Citizens would even take them on their travels. The first flat pack beds!

1865

Victorians invented bedsprings to use on wooden and metal frames, placing a mattress on top for comfort.

1990

The American space agency NASA invented memory foam, used today for pillows and mattresses.

2013

The first temperature controlled mattresses were developed.

1800

Cotton stuffed mattresses started to replace hay and feather.

1970

Foldaway Japanese futons (a padded mattress that can be rolled up) became popular around the world.

It will be exciting to see what's next for the evolution of beds.

1600

In Europe, ornately carved four-poster beds evolved, seen as a status symbol—the fancier the better!

2006

Yippee! The first bed with a TV attached was invented.

DON'T LET THE BEDBUGS BITE!

These bloodsucking beasties have lived in beds for thousands of years. Yikes!

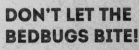

Vishnu

Hindus believe the supreme being Vishnu created the universe while in his cosmic sleep. Dreaming of a lotus flower growing from his belly button, the god Brahma emerged through the petals. Separating the flower into three parts, Brahma then created the heavens, the earth, and the sky.

milk

The Brownies

In British folklore, mysterious fairies called Brownies busied themselves with household chores while the residents slept. As payment, these elusive creatures were very fond of oatmeal and milk!

Baku

In Japanese folklore, Baku, a strange-looking mythical creature, had the trunk of an elephant, body of a bear, paws of a tiger, and tail of an ox. Known as a dream-eater, it would visit at night and gobble up all your nightmares!

Worry dolls

In Guatemala in Central America, children tell their worries to a handcrafted worry doll before going to bed. The doll then takes care of the worries during the night. Originating from the ancient Mayan tribes, the dolls are dressed in traditional Mayan clothing.

Hypnos

Hypnos (or in Latin, Somnus) is the Greek-Roman god of sleep. The son of Nyx (night), he lived in the underworld surrounded by his many sons who were the bringers of dreams.

Morpheus

One of Hypnos' sons, Morpheus was a dream messenger, while his brother Phobetor was the bringer of nightmares in animal and monster form. Phantasos, the third brother, was the creator of surreal and weird dreams.

MYTHS AND LEGENDS

Nighttime can be mysterious and spooky. With so many different faiths and beliefs, it's not surprising that some of the world's myths and legends can be rather extraordinary, charming, eerie, and even a little creepy! Some Japanese people believe if you can't sleep, it's because you are awake in someone else's dream—eek!

Myths and legends continued...

Moe'uhane

In the Hawaiian language, Moe'uhane means soul sleep. Ancient Hawaiians believed the gods would send them messages of guidance while they slept bringing luck, fortune in love, prophecies, and cures.

Sandman

In European folklore, a sandman puts you to sleep, then sprinkles magical sand in your eyes to inspire and encourage beautiful dreams. Ever had crusty corners in your eyes when you wake? It could be the magic sand!

Dream catcher

The dream catcher was the creation of the Ojibwe Tribe (meaning original people) in North America. They believed Asibikaashi, the Spider Woman, would protect and bring the sunlight to them unharmed by creating a web to catch bad dreams—with a hole in the middle for the good dreams to pass through.

The giant turtle

The Abenaki, a Native American tribe and First Nation believed the giant spirit—Creator of the World—made the earth on the back of a giant turtle just before sleeping. While asleep, he then created all the people and the animals.

Dreamtime

The Aboriginal people of Australia believe dreaming is when past, present, and future coexist.

SLEEP PARALYSIS

There is a condition called sleep paralysis—when you have been jolted awake in REM sleep, the brain keeps dreaming and your body is still paralyzed, making the hallucination more real and very scary. That could explain where all the scary nighttime legends come from!

3 a.m.

Legend has it that the witching hour is between 3 a.m.-4 a.m. when all the ghastly ghosts and spirits come out to play ...

Boo!

Scary myths include Mara, an evil spirit from Germanic folklore who sits on your chest and turns your dreams into nightmares. Mara or Mare is the origin of the word nightmare. The Night Hag is another terrifying legend—a supernatural creature who sits on the end of your bed being all evil and nasty.

THE NIGHT SKY

Looking up into a clear night sky can be awe-inspiring. Sleeping under the stars is a delight, the sheer vastness mind-boggling. Next time you go to bed, why not gaze up into the sky and wonder—like past philosophers and scientists—at the mysteries it holds.

DIFFERENT SKIES

The Northern Hemisphere sees different stars than the Southern Hemisphere.

Light pollution

In today's fast-paced world, our cities and towns are full of light, even at night. It may extend the day and keep us safe, but there is a downside. Since our bodies follow a body clock, light at the wrong time disturbs that pattern, causing many people to have sleep problems.

The stars

There are over 300 billion stars in our galaxy alone. Constellations, or group of stars, form patterns in the sky. Throughout history, civilizations used the stars to tell great stories about their gods. They also used them to navigate—like a map.

Night singers

Streetlights make some birds think it is daytime. They continue to sing even when they should be tucked up on their perch!

Perseus

The constellation Perseus, found in the northern sky, is named after the Greek mythological hero who slew the evil gorgon Medusa in her sleep. It was said she could turn any living thing to stone just by looking at it.

The moon

Over thousands of years, humans have believed that the lunar cycles can affect our moods and our sleep. But can the moon really affect how well we sleep? Some studies have shown when there is a full moon it can take longer to fall asleep and we might feel restless and have weird dreams. Yet other investigations have found no link between the two. It seems the mystery will stay with us a bit longer. How do you sleep on a full moon?

HUMANS AND SLEEP

Bed buddies

Two thirds of cats sleep with their human companions.

As you grow up, your relationship with sleep changes. How much we need evolves as our bodies and brains develop. While newborns seem to sleep forever and teenagers always seem to want to sleep in, our parents and grandparents need and get much less sleep— sometimes too little with the fast pace of modern life.

Countries around the world also have slightly different sleep schedules. In New Zealand children can be tucked up in bed by 7:30 p.m., whereas youngsters in Hong Kong average a bedtime three hours later!

NIGHT WORK

Millions of people around the world work at night. These can be jobs that are done 24 hours a day, jobs that can only be done at night, and important jobs that keep the world turning! From law enforcement, shelf stockers, and factory workers to delivery drivers, bartenders, and air traffic controllers! So how does that affect their sleep when we are hot wired to snooze at night?

Pilot

Some pilots prefer to fly at night as it can be really peaceful. To help them stay awake, many pilots keep bright lights on in the cockpits, which keeps them alert.

Firefighter

Firefighters work very irregular shift patterns and have to be mentally and physically ready to tackle any crisis at a moment's notice. Many suffer from some form of sleep disorder without even realizing it.

Nurse

Nurses must stay fully focused while monitoring sleeping patients on long night shifts. A sleep routine with a darkened room helps them get their all important rest. There are an estimated 28 million nurses in the world.

Astronaut

It's not easy sleeping in space! While orbiting the planet every 90 minutes, astronauts experience light and dark very differently than on planet Earth. This disrupts their sleep patterns and is where their eye masks come in handy!

TICKTOCK

Going to bed at the same time every day—regardless of the time—is the best way to combat sleep issues with nighttime working.

SLEEP TAILS

Salvador Dali

Artist Dali believed the secret to unlocking creativity was to sleep no longer than one second at a time. He slept holding a metal key—when he nodded off it would fall and wake him up.

Manufacturing

Global business works 24 hours a day to meet high demand, meaning many employees need to work at night. When returning home it is crucial the family member can have a quiet sleep even if everyone else is awake.

Shaquille O'Neal

Basketball legend O'Neal suffers from sleep apnea. This condition causes the sleeper to snore and even stop breathing for a few seconds! There are many reasons this can happen, including having a large tongue!

Emergency Doctor

Unpredictable, demanding, and frequently a matter of life and death, the emergency department requires a cool head even at 2 a.m. Thank goodness for these awesome medics!

Mary Shelley

While having a lucid dream (a dream where you know that you are dreaming), Shelley saw a vision of a monster. Quickly she opened her eyes, terrified, and started writing her most famous work—*Frankenstein*.

Sleeping with pets

In the United States, a whopping 71% of people love sleeping with their pets!

Igloo

Indigenous peoples have built igloos for centuries to shelter from the harsh Arctic weather while hunting. They are made of blocks of snow in a round shape, creating a self-supporting, cozy dome.

NORTH AMERICA

Hammock

Invented by the native inhabitants of Central and South America, many people in Mexico and South America still use hammocks as their main bed of choice today.

EUROPE

CENTRAL AMERICA

SPACE SNOOZE

To be able to get a good night's sleep, astronauts in space have to attach their sleeping bags to the walls and the ceilings of the space craft to stop themselves floating away!

SOUTH AMERICA

Tree houses

People have slept in tree dwellings for hundreds of years, from Asia right across the world to South America. You can still sleep in one today—how cool!

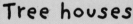

10 P.M.

Argentina in South America has one of the latest bedtimes for children around the world. They go to bed when their parents do!

ANTARCTICA

The great outdoors

Exploring the wilds of nature is thrilling and exciting. Adventurers report getting some of their best nights' sleep tucked up in a simple sleeping bag.

Kang bed-stove

The Kang is a brick-based platform used for many centuries in Northern China. It is still used today for working on, entertaining, and sleeping—the bricks are heated to keep it nice and warm.

Siesta

The Spanish tradition of an afternoon nap dates back thousands of years. People would nap to shelter from the heat.

ASIA

So high!

Mount Everest is the highest place on earth a human has slept. It is more difficult to sleep in high altitudes because of the lack of oxygen.

Pods

A capsule hotel from Japan consists of lots of individual pods about the size of a single bed. A great place to snooze unless you are claustrophobic!

Super nets

Since the year 2000, simple, insecticide-treated bed nets used in places like Africa and Asia have saved over 450 million lives from the deadly disease malaria, carried by biting mosquitoes.

AFRICA

OCEANIA

HOW AND WHERE

We don't just sleep in beds, there are lots of different places to sleep! We sleep in tents while camping, in cabins on boats—even up trees! Hammocks are not just for the beach, either. Ancient ways of sleeping have endured through time with many examples still used today.

ANTARCTICA

HOW MUCH SLEEP?

The amount of sleep we need does vary from person to person,
but what we do know is children need much more sleep than adults.
And as we get much older the amount of sleep we might need gets less.
So what are the right sleep recommendations for your age group?

IN A MINUTE

We are the only mammals
that consciously put off
going to sleep.

30%

of children around
the world report
sleep problems
every night!

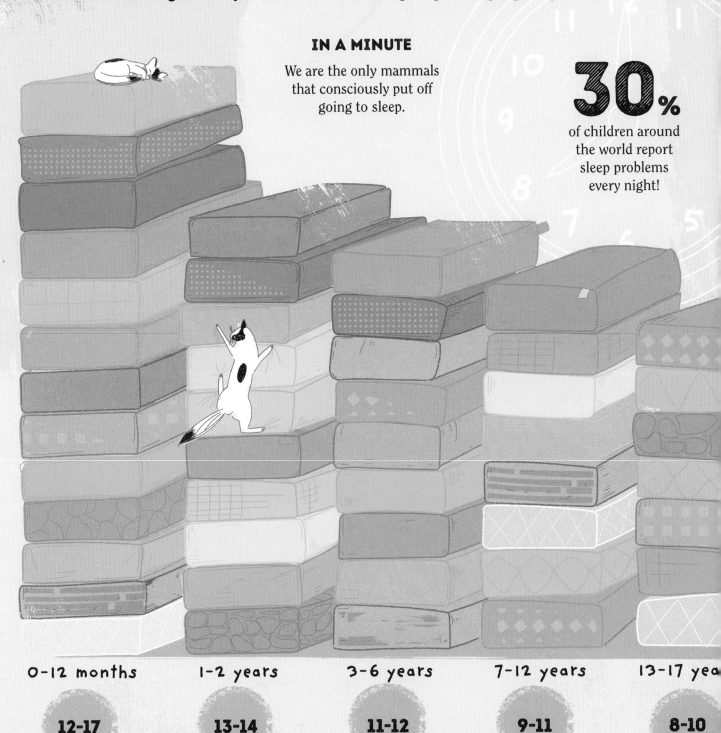

0-12 months	1-2 years	3-6 years	7-12 years	13-17 years
12-17	13-14	11-12	9-11	8-10

Recommended number of hours of sleep per day for each age group.

Anxiety

Feeling like you are not getting enough sleep can lead to anxious feelings and make you worry about going to bed. These thoughts are very common.

Napping

Regular daytime napping can help younger children give their bodies and minds time to rest and recharge. As children get older, a nap can help if you have had a terrible night's sleep or if you feel tired, but keep it short—no more than 30 minutes.

18-64 years	65+ years
7-9	7-8

QUIZ

Are you getting enough sleep?

1. **When you wake up how do you feel?**

a. Refreshed and ready for the day.
b. A little tired, but ok after breakfast.
c. Terrible, I feel SO tired and continue to feel sleepy throughout the day.

2. **Do you forget things?**

a. No, especially if they are important.
b. Sometimes.
c. What's my name again?

3. **Do you get irritated and angry?**

a. No, not really.
b. Sometimes, if I feel tired.
c. Yes, why is EVERYONE so annoying?

4. **Do you find it hard to concentrate?**

a. No, I have the focus of a hawk!
b. Sometimes when I start to daydream.
c. What was the question again?

5. **How many hours do you sleep?**

a. Between 9-12 hours.
b. Between 8-10 hours.
c. Less than 8.

Answer:
Mostly As   Plenty—a super-duper sleeper
Mostly Bs   Borderline—could get more.
Mostly Cs   You really need more zzz ...

-11 -10 -9 -8 -7 -6 -5 -4 -3 -2 -1 0

DATELINE

MERIDIAN LINE

ANCHORAGE~
Jakarta

Anchorage

Anchorage in Alaska is 15 hours behind Jakarta, the capital city of Indonesia.

Montreal~
NEW DELHI

The Canadian city of Montreal is 9.5 hours behind Delhi in India.

NORTH AMERICA

Montreal

New York City

London

P

Los Angeles

LA PAR

Los Angeles~
Paris ✈

Los Angeles in California is 9 hours behind Paris, France.

Mexico City

CENTRAL AMERICA

Lima

SOUTH AMERICA

Rio de Janeiro

THE MAP OF SLEEP

Since it is daytime on one side of the earth and nighttime on the other because the earth rotates around the sun, the world is divided into 24 time zones, starting at 0 hours in Greenwich in London, England. This is called UTC (Coordinated Universal Time). Shall we find out who might be awake when you are fast asleep?

-11 -10 -9 -8 -7 -6 -5 -4 -3 -2 -1 0

+2 +3 +4 +5 +6 +7 +8 +9 +10 +11 +12

Moscow—LIMA

Moscow in Russia is 8 hours ahead of the capital city of Peru, Lima.

WHAT TIME IS IT?

Our body clocks become confused when traveling through different time zones—this is called jet lag. Traveling east is more likely to cause sleep problems. Why? Our internal clock actually follows a 24.5 hour timer. So if you travel east you lose more time!

EUROPE

Moscow

ASIA

Shanghai—*Rio de Janeiro*

Shanghai in China is 11 hours ahead of Rio de Janeiro in Brazil.

Tokyo

Shanghai

New Delhi

AFRICA

Jakarta

TOKYO— NEW YORK

Tokyo in Japan is 13 hours ahead of New York City.

DATELINE

CAPE TOWN— MEXICO CITY

★★★★   ★★★★

In Cape Town, South Africa, it is 7 hours ahead of Mexico City in Mexico.

Can you find where you live on the map?

Sydney   OCEANIA

Sydney ~ LONDON

Sydney, Australia, is 9 hours ahead of London, UK.

+2 +3 +4 +5 +6 +7 +8 +9 +10 +11 +12

SLEEP IN NATURE

King of the slumber

Cats can spend over 16 hours a day "catnapping"! This is not all deep sleep, however—the smell of their food or call of their owner will usually get their attention!

While it is impossible to prove that every creature sleeps, most non-human animals do take some form of rest. With so many dangers lurking, many animals sleep literally with one eye open, and others will go long periods of time without sleep just to keep their babies safe.

Others have adapted to sleep in groups, like meerkats, who have lookouts to guard their snoozing family. Possibly the cutest example of sleep security is from the sea otter. They hold paws with each other while drifting on the sea surface, sometimes up to a hundred individual otters—like a furry raft!

Mallard duck

Ever noticed ducks sleeping in a row? Look closely and you will spot the ducks on each end keeping a watchful eye, so the middle birds can snooze in peace.

Wandering albatross

The wandering albatross can travel around the globe in just 46 days, snatching sleep while it flies.

Hanging parrots

Also known as bat parrots, hanging parrots doze upside down, hidden in the leaves.

Wren

Small birds like wrens snuggle together at night to keep warm. Once, 63 wrens were found sleeping in one small nest box!

Baby owls

Owlets spend more time in REM sleep than adult birds, which is good for their brain development.

Zebra finch

Australian zebra finches sing while they dream!

Alpine swift

These birds eat, drink, and sleep while flying, spending up to seven months at a time in the air.

Most birds travel at night when they migrate. So when do they sleep? It seems they reverse their sleep patterns, taking hundreds of naps during the day rather than one long bout of sleep at night.

Great frigate bird

Recent studies have shown that frigate birds take ten second napping bursts while flying nonstop for weeks. The master of the power nap!

Rock pigeon

The humble pigeon can do back flips in mid-air, ride the subway, and sleep with one eye open. What a cool bird!

Swainson's thrush

This thrush flies 3,000 miles to South America every year. It flies nonstop at night, and during the day it forages for food and takes hundreds of quick power naps!

SKY

Some birds can sleep while flying, others lock their talons on a perch so they don't fall off while taking a nap. Other birds can sleep with one eye open to watch for predators and can even keep half their brain active while the other side recharges in sleep!

LAND

Humans follow a monophasic sleep: one long slumber each night. But many animals follow a polyphasic sleep pattern, resting for lots of short periods throughout the day and night.

Black bear

Bears don't really hibernate. Why? Because their bodies are just too big! Instead they go into a deep sleep called a torpor. This conserves energy, but they can wake up quickly if disturbed!

Butterfly

Butterflies do rest, but they don't shut their eyes because they have no eyelids!

Lion

The greatest catnappers of them all, lions can snooze up to 20 hours a day! Males sleep more than females, who do most of the hunting.

Hairy armadillo

These armored sleep champions spend 18–20 hours a day snoozing in their burrows.

Ape

At night, apes love to curl up in a comfy tree-top bed made of leaves and twigs.

Bullfrog

Bullfrogs can go without sleep for months! They do take a few rests, but always remain alert.

Koala

A koala's diet is mostly made up of eucalyptus leaves, which take ages to digest. That might explain why they sleep slumped on a branch for up to 22 hours!

Snake

Snakes never close their eyes. It makes it hard to tell if a snake is snoozing or watching its next meal ... eek!

Fly

A fly's sleep pattern is similar to a human's. They can become sleep deprived if they don't get enough rest, the babies sleep more than adults, and they even take afternoon naps.

Bee

Tired bumblebees sleep on the job! You can sometimes find them snoozing inside the head of a flower.

Horse

Horses usually sleep standing up, but they do lie down for short periods to catch up on REM sleep.

Giraffe

The tallest animal in the world has the shortest amount of sleep. It clocks an average of 30 minutes a day, sleeping in five minute bursts.

Ant

Worker ants take power naps, sometimes as many as 250 a day! The queen, however, will snooze for a good nine hours.

Queen ant

Mole

Moles are very industrious and follow a pattern of four hours' work and four hours' sleep, all day every day.

Rabbit

Rabbits sleep in their burrows in the daytime, becoming active at dawn and dusk. Their teeth and nails never stop growing!

Wombat

Found in Australia, the wombat sleeps for 16 hours a day! They can run almost as fast as Usain Bolt!

Eurasian badger

Badgers live in lots of chambers called a sett, where they sleep tucked up with their clan during the day. They love a tidy house, and often replace their bedding or bring it outside to air.

Meerkat

Meerkats love to snuggle up in their burrows, piling on top of one another in a heap! The ruling female always sleeps at the bottom.

Earthworms

When it gets dry, earthworms sleep curled up in a tight ball inside a slime-lined, underground chamber.

Periodical cicada

This species of cicada sleeps underground for 17 years!

Jerboa

The cute little jerboa lives in the desert. It sleeps during the daytime in burrows sealed with a plug of sand, which helps keep the heat out and the moisture in.

Fennec fox

Living in the deserts of North Africa, these tiny, bat-eared foxes sleep in the cool of their den, hidden away from the fierce heat outside. Their fur helps keep them cool, and they have furry feet that look like little boots!

UNDERGROUND

Many animals sleep underground throughout the year. But in winter, their sleep pattern can change when they go into a state of suspended animation, known as hibernation. This is more than just a deep sleep; it saves energy and helps the animals survive the winter months.

UNDERWATER

Sea creatures have developed special ways of snoozing underwater. Fish sleep with their eyes open, while some sharks nap in the path of ocean currents.

Sea otter

These cute creatures sleep drifting on the sea surface, wrapped in kelp seaweed blankets.

Sperm whale

These whales sleep in groups known as pods. They snooze vertically for a few minutes at a time, bobbing underwater like giant corks.

Octopus

These tentacled marvels have been known to enter REM sleep—this means they may have octopus dreams!

Parrot fish

This strange fish covers itself with mucus when it goes to sleep, creating a snot-bubble sleeping bag.

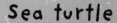

Sea turtle

Sea turtles can hold their breath for hours while snoozing on the ocean floor.

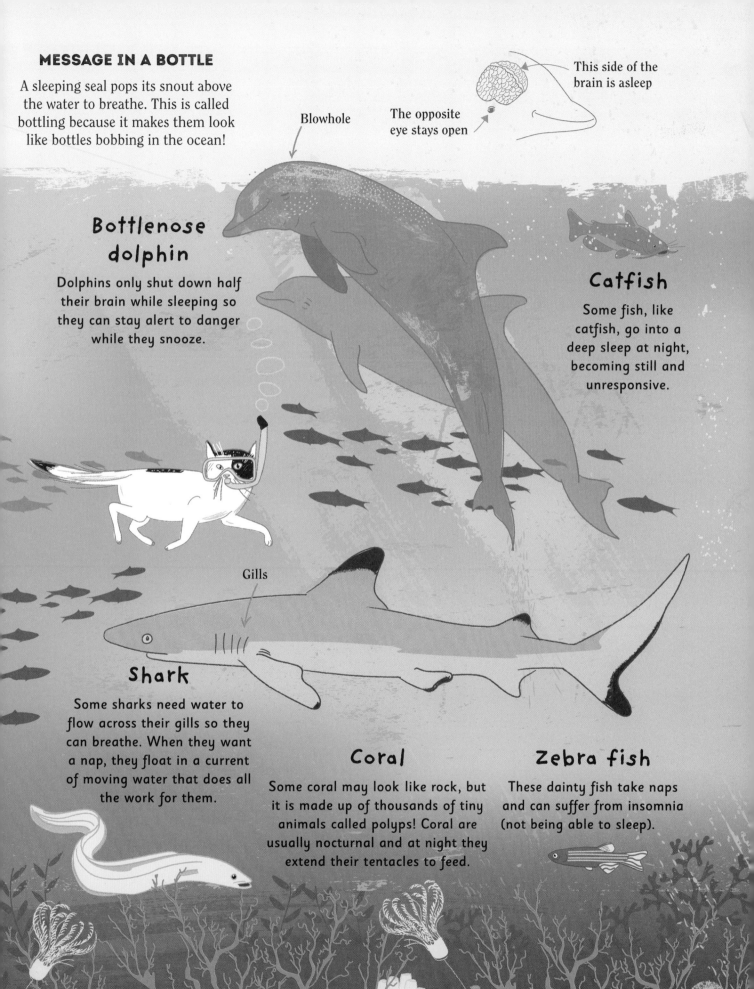

MESSAGE IN A BOTTLE

A sleeping seal pops its snout above the water to breathe. This is called bottling because it makes them look like bottles bobbing in the ocean!

Blowhole

The opposite eye stays open

This side of the brain is asleep

Bottlenose dolphin

Dolphins only shut down half their brain while sleeping so they can stay alert to danger while they snooze.

Catfish

Some fish, like catfish, go into a deep sleep at night, becoming still and unresponsive.

Gills

Shark

Some sharks need water to flow across their gills so they can breathe. When they want a nap, they float in a current of moving water that does all the work for them.

Coral

Some coral may look like rock, but it is made up of thousands of tiny animals called polyps! Coral are usually nocturnal and at night they extend their tentacles to feed.

Zebra fish

These dainty fish take naps and can suffer from insomnia (not being able to sleep).

WHO'S AWAKE?

While we're tucked up cozy in bed, some creatures are just waking up. To survive in the darkness, nocturnal animals have more developed senses, such as smell and hearing. Some also have huge eyes to help them navigate the nighttime world.

Coyote

Coyotes have adapted to living in many cities in North America, coming out mainly at night to avoid humans.

Bat

There are over 1,400 species of bats. During the day, bats sleep upside down in dark, cool places like inside caves and under bridges.

Firefly

The firefly glows in the dark! It flies at night, flashing its lit belly in a pattern to attract a mate. Despite its name, this bug is actually a beetle and is about the size of a paperclip.

Tiger

As an ambush predator, tigers hunt at night when the darkness helps them stay hidden from their prey. After eating, they then snooze for up to 18 hours, sleeping off their big meal!

Pangolin

Some of the endangered pangolin species sleep in underground burrows during the day while others sleep in trees.

Scorpion

All scorpions glow under ultraviolet light like moonlight.

Pteropus

These giant bats live in huge numbers, hanging from trees in groups. With big, cute eyes, they feast on pollen, nectar, and fruits.

Owl monkey

Also known as night monkeys, these animals are the only nocturnal primates in the world. They have huge, round eyes to see in the dark.

Barn owl

Owls use their acute hearing to locate prey in the pitch black of night.

Spectacled bear

These bears get their name from the circles of light fur around their eyes. They build snooze platforms in the trees where they sleep in the daylight hours

Cockroach

These scurrying beasties are active at night, and while they don't sleep like humans do, they enter a period of sleep-like motionlessness for a while every day.

Raccoon

These nocturnal critters spend the nights foraging and will eat anything, from berries to burgers!

Slug

These nighttime munchers have up to 27,000 teeth!

BEE-ING CLEVER

Honey bees learn while they sleep. During their 5–8 hour daily snooze, their brains store long-term memories—just like us!

Slowing time

Having your home on your own back can be very handy, especially if you fancy a long nap. The snail can sleep for a whopping three years, prompted by a lack of moisture in its environment.

Giraffe

Elephant

Goat

Pig

Donkey

Fruit fly

Honey bee

TIMELINE

| 30 min | 2.5 hours | 3 | 4 | 6 |

Generally, meat-eating predators such as lions and tigers sleep much more than bigger plant-eating animals, such as giraffes and elephants, and prey animals such as sheep and goats. Reptiles like the bearded dragon lizard experience a staggering 350 sleep cycles a night, lasting 80 seconds each.

SLEEP IN NUMBERS

Sleep patterns in the animal kingdom vary greatly. One of the tallest animals sleeps for only 30 minutes a day, while one of the smallest snoozes more than 20 hours at a time ...

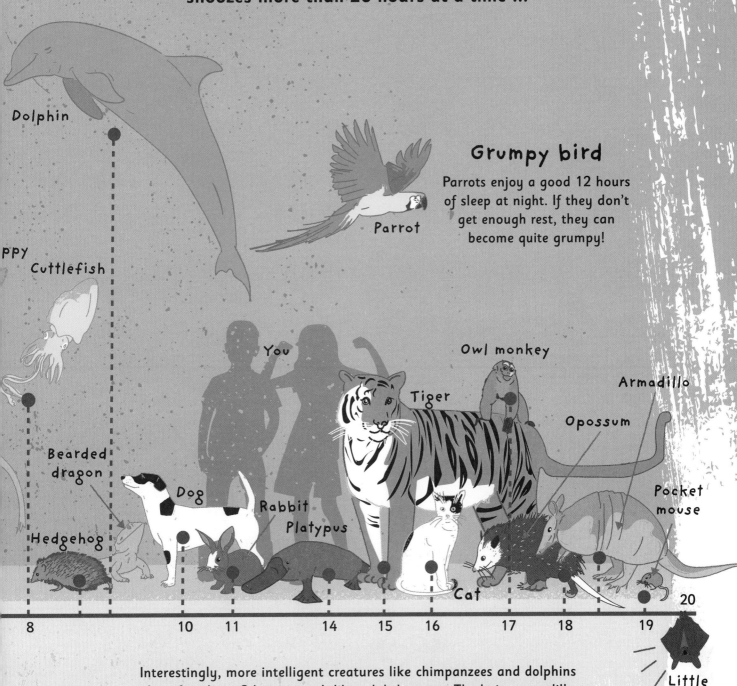

Grumpy bird

Parrots enjoy a good 12 hours of sleep at night. If they don't get enough rest, they can become quite grumpy!

Dolphin

Parrot

PPY Cuttlefish

You

Owl monkey

Armadillo

Tiger

Opossum

Bearded dragon

Dog

Rabbit

Platypus

Pocket mouse

Hedgehog

Cat

8   10 11   14   15   16   17   18   19   20

Little brown bat

Interestingly, more intelligent creatures like chimpanzees and dolphins sleep for about 8 hours, much like adult humans. The hairy armadillo sleeps for up to 20 hours at a time—unsurprising as it has to lug around its heavy shell which is three times its body weight. Oof!

PLANTS

Just like us, plants respond to light and dark. Many plants shut down when it gets dark, and then snack on the glucose (sugar) they create from the sunlight. Many plants, like tulips or hibiscus, need at least six hours of direct sunlight a day to flower.

Moonflower

Shaped like a full moon, this flower only blooms at night. Its heavy scent attracts night moths for pollination.

Orchid

The orchid has a growing cycle followed by a dormant phase, just like a long sleep.

Crocus

Many plants—such as crocuses and hibiscuses—close their petals tight at night.

Hibiscus

PHOTOSYNTHESIS

Plants process energy from sunlight, water, and carbon dioxide in the air. At night this process stops and the plants conserve energy very much like sleep.

Passiflora

Some plants can help us sleep. This flower, also known as the passionflower, is used for medicine to calm anxiety and give restful sleep.

Golden Pothos

This hanging plant cleans the air of harmful toxins, which can give us a better night's sleep.

Christmas cactus

The Christmas cactus needs 12–14 hours of darkness to create flower buds. As the name suggests, they bloom just in time for the Christmas season.

Tulip

TIPS FOR BETTER SLEEP

Feline focus

Cats really are four-legged masters of meditation. Their purrs are like a calming chant.

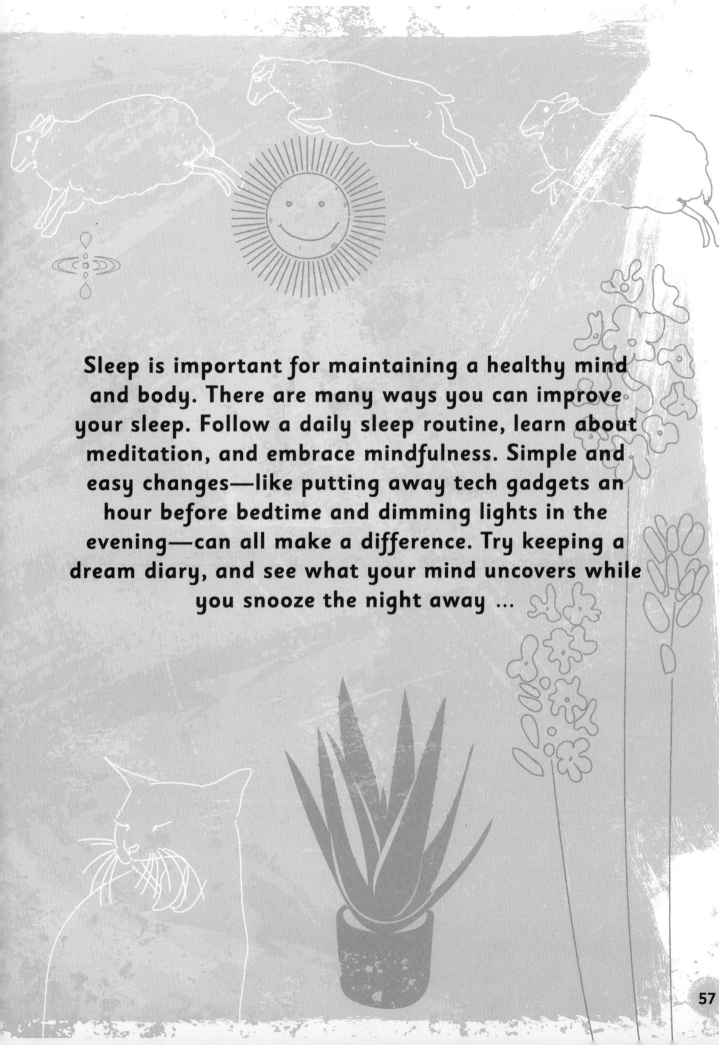

Sleep is important for maintaining a healthy mind and body. There are many ways you can improve your sleep. Follow a daily sleep routine, learn about meditation, and embrace mindfulness. Simple and easy changes—like putting away tech gadgets an hour before bedtime and dimming lights in the evening—can all make a difference. Try keeping a dream diary, and see what your mind uncovers while you snooze the night away ...

TRUE OR FALSE

How many facts about sleep are really true?

You can swallow eight spiders a year while sleeping!

25% of children experience insomnia.

FALSE

A total myth! Spiders would not go anywhere near an open mouth!

TRUE

Approximately a quarter of all children will have sleep problems at some point in their childhood.

Yawning is contagious

15% of humans in the world sleepwalk.

TRUE

Even reading the word "yawn" can make you yawn! (Did you just yawn while reading this?)

TRUE

Sleepwalking can run in the family.

1 in 8 people dream in black and white.

TRUE

However, a big dog's dreams last longer than a small doggy's dreams.

TRUE

Even more people used to dream in black and white before the invention of the color television.

Small dogs dream more than big dogs.

TRUE

Much like some people talk in their sleep, some people sign instead!

Some people who are deaf use sign language when they sleep!

Daily exercise can help you sleep better.

FALSE

But if you go to bed with a full tummy, you may get more vivid dreams.

TRUE

Even 30 minutes a day (not too close to bedtime!) will make a difference in the quality of your sleep.

Eating cheese before bed gives you nightmares.

MINDFULNESS

Mindfulness is a really simple technique that can help us focus on what we are doing right now—paying attention to our thoughts and feelings without judging them. Meditation can really help you achieve this.

SLEEP AND MEDITATION

Regular meditation not only calms the mind but can make us feel better overall. It can minimize anxiety and help us feel happier. It can also help make us smarter, increase our attention span, and boost creativity. As an added bonus, we fall asleep faster and have a better night's sleep. Meditation can boost the sleep hormone melatonin and increase serotonin, the natural chemical that promotes wellness and happiness.

Bedtime meditation

Get comfortable and snuggle up in your bed.
Take deep breaths—in through your nose, then out through your mouth.

Place your hands on your stomach. When you breathe in deep, feel your
tummy expanding like a balloon. Breathe out and feel your tummy go down.
Repeat 3 times.
This gets much easier with practice.

Notice your bed beneath you. Feel yourself sinking into the soft pillows
and mattress, all warm and safe. The walls of your bedroom protecting you—
nothing will disturb your peace. Feel calm, feel secure,
ready to drift off …

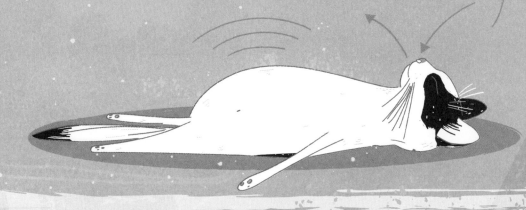

Tip

**Don't worry if your mind wanders, just say hello to
those thoughts and go back to your breathing.**

Take a mindful moment

Close your eyes and imagine you are in a beautiful, relaxing place. Maybe a meadow
full of flowers, or a beach with gentle, lapping waves. Imagine the sounds you
would hear, the smell of the air—picture as much detail as you can. Notice how
your breathing begins to slow as you start to relax …

If you keep practicing this visualization, it will become easier
to relax every time you go back to your imaginary special place.

CREATE YOUR OWN DREAM JOURNAL

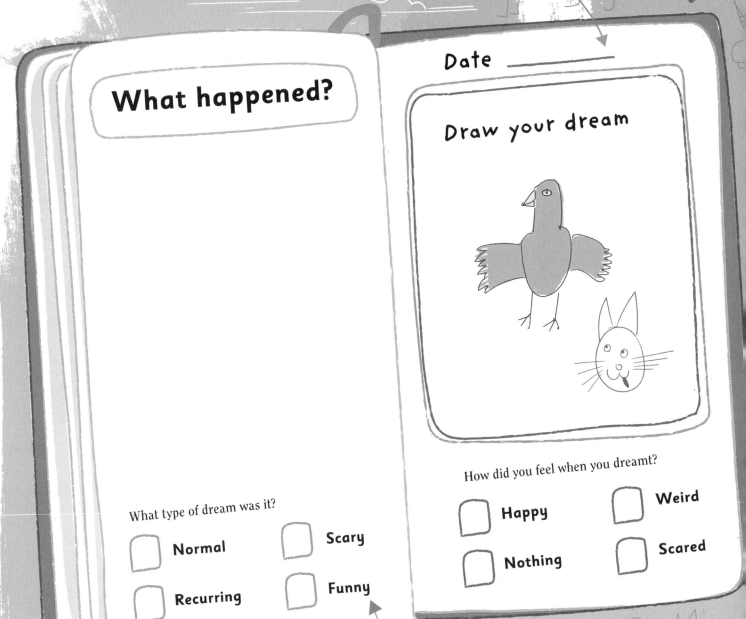

What happened?

What type of dream was it?

☐ Normal   ☐ Scary

☐ Recurring   ☐ Funny

Date _____

Draw your dream

How did you feel when you dreamt?

☐ Happy   ☐ Weird

☐ Nothing   ☐ Scared

Keep your journal next to your bed with a pencil or pen to record your dreams when you wake up.

YESTERDAY

Paul McCartney, from the band The Beatles, composed the tune to "Yesterday" in a dream, and wrote it down as soon as he woke up.

How to record dreams

1. Write down anything you can remember from your dreams.

2. Do a doodle of what you saw or felt.

3. Record the date to track your dreams.

4. Have you had this dream before?

5. How does it make you feel?

DREAM JOURNAL

A dream journal is a type of diary you use to record your dreams. Simply write and draw what you dreamt about as soon as you wake up. See if you can spot any patterns—it could help solve some of your worries you might not even know you have!

PRACTICAL TiPS

Here are a few easy tips you can try to get an even better night's slumber. Create your own routine that will set you up for years of fantastic sleep.

1. Nature

Nature has a positive effect on our mental health. Spending time outside in green spaces will do wonders for your mood and sleep. Go on—go out and hug a tree!

2. Smell

Some scents can help you sleep. Lavender is very soothing, great when you want to relax. Rose, valerian, and vanilla are some other beautiful, sleep-inducing smells you can try in your bedroom.

3. Routine

1. Keep it cool. The perfect temperature for snoozing is 64°F (18°C).

2. Make your bed every morning.

3. Give yourself a regular sleep and wake time.

4. Softer lighting in the evening.

4. Napping

The ideal nap is about 20 minutes long and shouldn't be taken too late in the afternoon. However, preschoolers can nap up to two hours. If you often feel sleepy in the afternoon, it may mean that you should be going to bed earlier.

Cats are the world's experts in napping.

SOOTHING SOUNDS

Music at 60 beats per minute helps you sleep, because it's the same rhythm as a resting heartbeat.

6. Food

Some foods contain tryptophan—an amino acid that promotes sleep. If you need a snack before bedtime, try some of these sleep-friendly options.

Yogurt

Oats

Peanut butter on toast

Bananas

Peanut butter on toast contains both carbohydrates and protein— a great sleepy combo.

Bananas are an excellent source of magnesium and potassium.

5.

Sunshine

Getting enough sunshine helps the body produce vitamin D and suppress melatonin, keeping you wide awake during the day— which is essential for good sleep at night.

7. Houseplants

Plants can have relaxing and purifying effects. Some even remove toxic chemicals from the air. Improving air quality will promote better health and sleep.

Spider plant

Snake plant

Aloe vera

8. Bath

Enjoy at hot soak before bed—it helps you fall asleep faster by lowering your body temperature just in time for bed.

9. Bedtime breathing

Try these four simple breathing routines to calm the mind before bedtime.

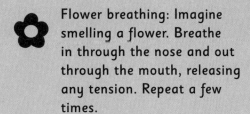

Flower breathing: Imagine smelling a flower. Breathe in through the nose and out through the mouth, releasing any tension. Repeat a few times.

Bear breathing: Breathe just like a snoozing bear. Inhale through the nose—pause—count 1 2 3—exhale—count 1 2 3 ... then repeat.

Bunny breathing: Imagine being a rabbit! Take three quick sniffs in the nose, then exhale one long breath out the nose. This is great for instant calm.

The hissing breath: Breathe in through the nose, long and deep—and out through the mouth with a hissing sound like a snake.

10. Stretching

A good stretch before bed can help release tension in your muscles.

1. The bear hug: Wrap your arms around yourself like a hug, grasping your shoulders for about 30 seconds. Release and stretch your arms wide. Switch arms and repeat.

2. The butterfly: Sit down and bring the soles of your feet together. Keep your spine straight and hold the position while you feel the gentle stretch.

3. Side stretch: Extend your left arm above your head while sitting. Place your right arm on the floor and lean to the right—keeping your left arm above your ear—hold. Repeat on the other side.

11. Gadgets

Switch off all screens at least one hour before bed. The blue light that shines from our devices can mess with the sleep hormone melatonin and stops us falling asleep. It can also cause anxiety.

Try to keep devices out of your bedroom.

TEXT ZZZS

Some people send text messages while they are fast asleep!

12. Hot drinks

A warm, milky drink with calcium helps your bones grow and your body produce sleep hormones. Yum!

ROUTINE

Routine is the key to an awesome night's sleep. Do the same relaxing things in the same order before bed every night to see the results!

13. Bedtime story

Reading or listening to a bedtime story every night really helps you sleep. It sets a routine and can help you de-stress after a busy day. Books really are the best!

Books really are paw-some!

GLOSSARY

ACUTE
Highly developed

AMBUSH
A surprise attack

APNEA
A condition that causes you to stop breathing for a few seconds while sleeping

ANXIETY
A feeling of worry or nervousness

ARMORED
Protected by armor

BASTET
Ancient Egyptian goddess of cats

CHRONOTYPE
A person's natural preferred time to sleep

CIRCADIAN
A naturally recurring twenty-four hour cycle (even without light or dark to show night and day)

CIVILIZATION
Society where people have built a complex city or country

CLAUSTROPHOBIC
An extreme fear of small, confined spaces

CONSCIOUSLY
To do something in a deliberate way

CONSTELLATION
A group of stars in a recognizable pattern

CONTAGIOUS
To spread from one person to another

DIURNAL
Active in the daytime

DREAMS
A series of thoughts and images seen in someone's mind while they are asleep

FOLKLORE
Traditional beliefs and stories passed down through generations by word of mouth

FORAGING
Searching for food and water

HALLUCINATION
Experiencing something that isn't really there

HAMMOCK
A bed made from a material like canvas and supported between two points by a piece of rope or cord.

HEMISPHERE
Half of the earth—northern or southern

HIBERNATION
Period of inactivity that some animals go through in the winter

INSECTICIDE
A chemical used to ward off insects

INSOMNIA
A condition where you find it difficult to sleep

LUCID DREAMS
A dream where you know that you are dreaming

MAGNESIUM
Magnesium supports a healthy immune system, helps your bones stay strong, and helps you maintain energy

MEDITATION
The act of meditating—concentrating to get to a clear and calm mind

MELATONIN
A hormone that your body makes. It can help control your sleep patterns.

MENTAL WELL-BEING
Your thoughts and feelings

MINDFULNESS
Being conscious and aware of your thoughts and feelings

MYTHS AND LEGENDS
Traditional stories

NAP
A short period of sleep, usually outside normal sleeping hours

NIGHTMARE
Sometimes called a "bad dream," a nightmare is an unpleasant dream that can cause you to feel fear or anxiety

NOCTURNAL
Active at night

PARALYZED
When the body is partly or completely incapable of movement

POTASSIUM
Potassium is an important mineral found in the body. When you don't have enough, it can make you feel weak and tired.

PROPHECY
A prediction of what could happen in the future.

REM SLEEP
Rapid Eye Movement Sleep—a unique, deep stage of the sleep cycle where you are more likely to dream vividly.

SIESTA
An afternoon rest or nap taken during the hottest hours of the day in a hot climate

STRESS
Feeling mentally or emotionally strained.

SUPERNATURAL
Something not explained by science or nature

TORPOR
A state of decreased activity that some animals go through to survive periods of reduced availability of their food sources

TRIGGERS
The cause of a particular event, feeling, or sensation

INDEX

A

Abenaki 27
Aboriginal people 27
albatrosses 42
Alcmaeon of Croton 20
aloe vera 65
alpine swifts 43
ancient Egypt 18, 20, 22
ancient Greece 20–21, 25, 28
ancient Hawaii 26
ancient Maya 24
ancient Northern Europe 22
ancient Rome 22, 25
ants 46
anxiety 36, 60, 67
apes 44
Argentina 34
armadillos 44, 53
Asibikaashi 26
astronauts 32
Australia 27

B

badgers 36
Baku 24
Bastet 18, 20
bats 50–51, 53
bearded dragons 53
bears 44, 51
beds 22–23, 34–35
bees 45, 52
biphasic sleep 21
body clock 8, 12
Bolt, Usain 46
bones 11, 13
brain 10, 12
Brahma 24

Britain 24
brownies 24
bullfrogs 44
butterflies 44

C

catfish 49
cats 4, 18, 30, 40, 53, 56, 64
China 35
Christmas cactus 55
chronotypes 8–9
cicadas 47
circadian rhythm 8
cockroaches 51
constellations 28–29
coral 49
coyotes 50
crocus 54
Ctesibius 21
cuttlefish 53

D

Dali, Salvador 33
digestive system 10
doctors 33
dogs 53, 59
dolphins 49, 53
donkeys 52
dream catcher 26
dreaming 13, 14–15, 16–17, 20, 59, 62–63
dream journal 62–63
dream tablets 20
ducks 42

E

elephants 52

Everest, Mount 35
eyes 10

F

fennec foxes 47
fetal position 7
firefighters 32
fireflies 50
fish 48–49, 52–53
flies 45, 52
France 23
Frankenstein 33
free-fall position 7
free radicals 12
futons 23

G

giraffes 45, 52
goats 52
golden pothos 55
great frigate bird 43
Guatemala 24
guppies 52

H

hammocks 34
Hawaii 26
hedgehogs 53
hibernation 44–45
hibiscus 54
Hinduism 24
history, myths, and legends 18–27
Hong Kong 31
horses 45
humans and sleep 30–39
hummingbird type 8
hypnic jerk 11
Hypnos 25

I

igloos 34
Indigenous peoples 26–27
insomnia 49, 58
Isis 18, 20

J

Japan 23, 24, 35
jerboas 47
jet lag 39

K

Kang bed-stove 35
kidneys 10
koalas 45

L

lark type 8
lavender 64
left-handedness 14
light pollution 28
lions 44, 52–53
log position 6
Louis XIV, King 23
lucid dreaming 33
lymph nodes 11

M

malaria 35
manufacturing 33
Mara 27
McCartney, Paul 62
medieval Christians 20–21
meditation 60–61
Medusa 29
meerkats 41, 47

melatonin 12, 60, 65, 67
memory 12–13, 15
memory foam 23
Mesopotamia 20
Mexico 34
Middle Ages, 20-21, 22
mice 53
migration 43
mindfulness 60–61
Moe-uhane 26
moles 46
monophasic sleep 21, 44
moon 29
moonflower 54
Morpheus 25
moths 54
muscles 11, 13, 66

N

napping 37
NASA 23
New Zealand 31
Night Hag 27
nightmares 16–17, 24–25, 59
night sky 28–29
night terrors 17
nocturnal animals 50–51
northern hemisphere 28
NREM 17
nurses 32
Nyx 25

O

octopuses 48
Ojibwe Tribe 26
O'Neal, Shaquille 33

opossums 53
orchids 54
owls 42, 51
owl monkeys 51, 53
owl type 9

P

Page, Larry 16
pangolins 50
parrot fish 48
parrots 42, 53
passiflora 55
Perseus 28
Phantasos 25
Phobetor 25
photosynthesis 55
pigs 52
pilots 32
plants 56–57, 65
platypuses 53
pod beds 35
polyphasic sleep 44
polyps 49
positions 6–7
pteropus 51

R

rabbits 46, 53
raccoons 51
REM 10–11, 13, 15, 27, 42, 45, 48
rock pigeons 43
rose 64

S

sandman 26
scorpions 50
seals 49
sea otters 41, 48
sea turtles 48
serotonin 60

sharks 49
sheep 52
Shelley, Mary 33
Sibudu Cave 22
siesta 35
sign language 59
skin 11
sleep apnea 33
sleep in nature 40–55
sleep paralysis 27
sleep spindles 12
sleepwalking 13, 58
snake plant 65
snakes 45
snails 52
sneezing 7
soldier position 6
South Africa 22
southern hemisphere 28
Spain 35
spider plant 65
spiders 58
stages of sleep 12–13
starfish position 6
stars 28–29
stomach 10
stretching 66
Swainson's thrush 43
swift type 9

T

tigers 50, 52-53
time zones 38-39
tips for better sleep 56–67
torpor 44
tryptophan 65
tulip 55

U

United States 34

V

valerian 64
vanilla 64
Victorians 23
Vishnu 24
vitamin D 65

W

whales 48
what is sleep? 4–17
wombats 46
woodcock type 9
worry dolls 24
wrens 42

Y

yawning 58
yearner position 7

Z

zebra finches 42
zebra fish 49

Mimi
(Sleep expert)

2004–2019

Vicky Woodgate

Moka
(Cat-nap champion)

About the author

Vicky Woodgate has been drawing for what seems like fur-ever …
From tiny illustrations to MASSIVE murals—all over the world. She
also loves to write about cool subjects and awesome facts and has
written two books already. She works from a studio on the south coast
of England and has lived with two sleep experts for years, Moka and
Mimi, who are the inspiration for our furry, four-legged sleep guide.

Thank you

For the coolest girls in Spain,
Dolly, Nancy, and Frida.

And to El my niece
and your pursuit of better sleep!

Thank you to Zoë
for your inspiration :)

And to the DK team past and present,
you have been PAW-SOME!

That's it for meow!

DK would like to thank the following:
Susie Rae for proofreading and indexing, Rituraj Singh for
picture research, and Vicki Dawson for consulting.

**The publisher would like to thank the following
for their kind permission to reproduce their photographs:**

(Key: a-above; b-below/bottom; c-center; f-far; l-left; r-right; t-top)

20 Alamy Stock Photo: The Picture Art Collection (cla). **Bridgeman Images:** ©
Zev Radovan (tr). 21 123RF.com: Antonio Abrignani (bl). **Alamy Stock Photo:**
Science History Images / Photo Researchers (crb). **22 Getty Images:** AFP /
Khaled Desouki (cb). **23 Getty Images:** De Agostini / DEA / G. Dagli Orti (bl).
25 Getty Images: Universal Images Group / Universal Images Group (t).
27 Dreamstime.com: Robert Spriggs (cl). **29 Science Photo
Library:** Sebastian Kaulitzki (tr). **58 Dorling Kindersley:** Jerry
Young (ca). **65 Dreamstime.com:** Andreadonetti (bl). **67
Dreamstime.com:** Axstokes (ca); Mikhail Matsonashvili
(tr); Fototocam (cra); Le Thuy Do (clb)

All other images © Dorling Kindersley
For further information see: www.dkimages.com